Baby
Zebu's Ears

Alana Zimmerman

ISBN | 9798360840473

BABY ZEBU

Late in September, under a cloudless sky, in a meadow peppered with butterflies, rays of sunshine basked the billowing blades of grass where a baby cow named Zebu was born. He was small with soft matted fur, mottled black and white. After Zebu was born and tried to stand, his Mom noticed that little baby Zebu's ears were pinned back.

Weeks after he was born, Zebu's ears were still pinned. Zebu's Mom tried to lick them to unpin them, and Zebu would rub his head against trees and bushes to try and unpin them, but they stubbornly refused to unpin. From that day on, all the meadow animals knew Zebu as the baby cow with pinned back ears.

Zebu accepted his pinned back ears and started to enjoy his life in the meadow. There were so many colors and smells that it overwhelmed him. He felt a sudden joy in his small heart that made his tentative steps firmer and made his little heart leap. He was such a happy baby cow. Even when it rained, he was happy. He would flick raindrops off of his tail or try to catch them on his tongue.

All of the animals in the meadow loved baby Zebu. He was an adorable, sweet, friendly, playful soul who always looked to help a fellow friend in need or stopped to say hello and chat. All of his friends would ask daily, "how are your ears doing Zebu, are they still pinned?" he would respond with a big smile and say, "doing just fine, and yes, they are still pinned."

Baby Zebu loved to roam the meadow and play, but he particularly loved to smell the flowers that grew on the side of the meadow. The small daisies and buttercups were especially vibrant, and he thought they smelled heavenly. Zebu loved to bury his head in them and enjoy their sweet fragrances almost daily.

Early one day as baby Zebu scampered about the meadow as he usually did, he noticed something strange. His hearing was always good, but this time it seemed even better. He could hear things happening many miles away and far below the ground. Zebu thought, well, I guess it is because my ears are pinned back. It must have given me special hearing.

One peaceful afternoon, baby Zebu scampered about
the meadow, burying his head in as many buttercups
and daisies as he could find when suddenly, he heard
a low rumble.

What was that sound? Where was it coming from? Zebu wondered.

Baby Zebu now had an odd feeling. It was unsettling and made him feel uneasy. He had seen storms before, but this felt different. He went to his Mom and tried to get her attention, but she was busy chewing cud.

Zebu found his friends, the worker ants, and tried to explain the uneasy feeling and the strange sound. Morty, the manager, kept yelling to his workers to keep up the progress they were making building the large ant hill they were behind schedule constructing. He did not have time for baby Zebu.

Down the bank towards the river Zebu found Hamilton, the hedgehog. Hamilton was out and about, scurrying around looking for his food supply for the day. He tended to hoard food in case of an emergency. Zebu tried to describe the sound and his anxious feeling, but Hamilton was too focused on food and had no time for baby Zebu.

After leaving Hamilton to his food
hoarding, Zebu continued his journey
to see Nigel, the beaver. Nigel was busy
shoring up his dam as he always did, but
Nigel was also very busy and did not have
time for baby Zebu.

As Zebu turned from Nigel and looked downstream he saw the otters, Klaus and Irma. They were frolicking in the water, cleaning themselves and floating on their backs, holding hands, getting ready to nap. Zebu remembered that otters hold hands when they sleep, so they do not drift away from one another. He always found that very endearing, but now he was frustrated since they didn't have time for him either. No one had time for him.

He heard the sound again and felt a faint wind, and saw dark clouds
approaching.

Zebu felt exasperated now. It felt like the temperature was getting warmer and the wind was picking up. He thought something did not feel right. He was a bit worried and wanted all of his friends to take shelter and be safe, but no one would give him any time or listen to him.

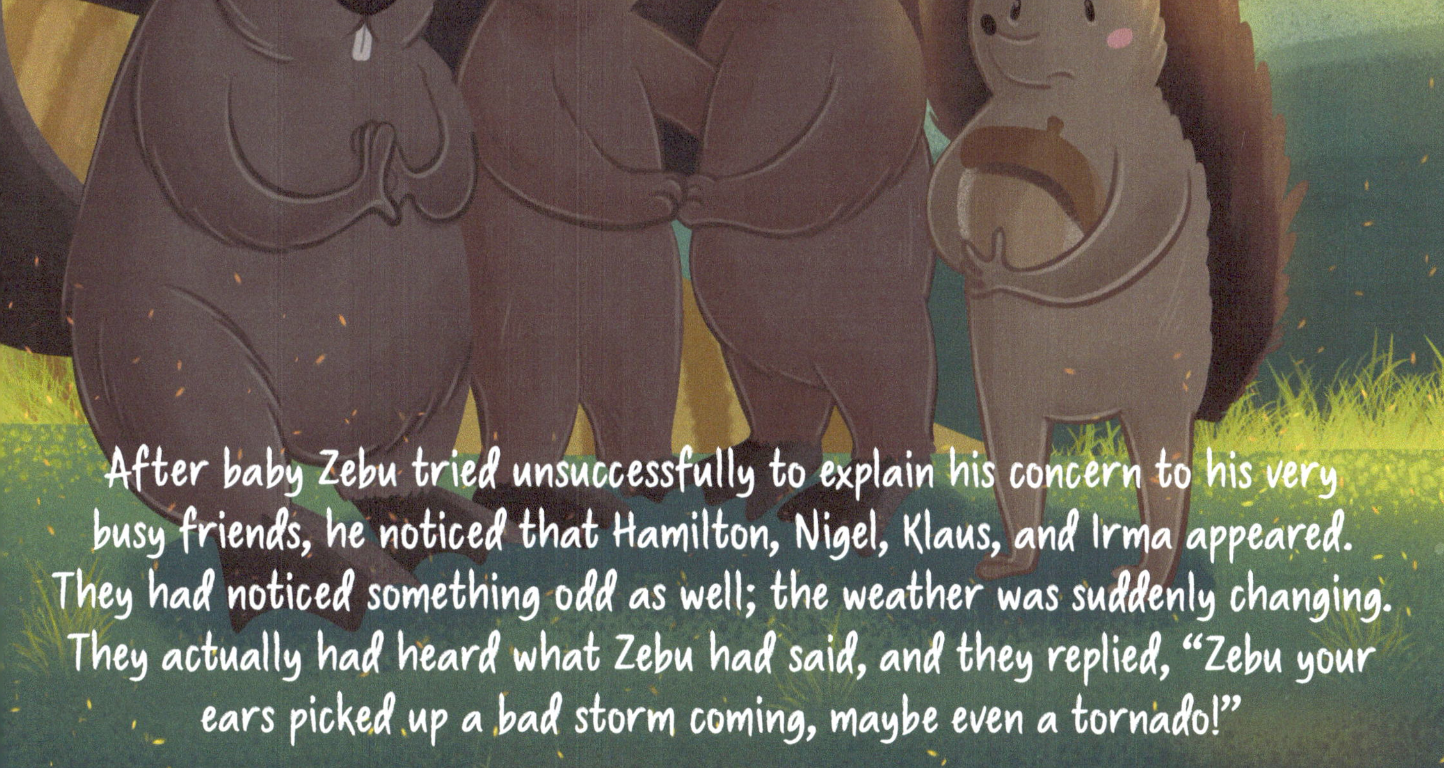

After baby Zebu tried unsuccessfully to explain his concern to his very busy friends, he noticed that Hamilton, Nigel, Klaus, and Irma appeared. They had noticed something odd as well; the weather was suddenly changing. They actually had heard what Zebu had said, and they replied, "Zebu your ears picked up a bad storm coming, maybe even a tornado!"

They all said together, "quick Zebu run and warn others. Tell them that your ears heard a very bad storm coming and to take cover."

Baby Zebu ran as fast as he could and yelled, "a storm is coming, run, take shelter!!"

As everyone took cover, a storm took hold. Rain, wind, thunder, and lightning struck and were so loud that it frightened many of the animals.

Suddenly, there was a roar, and the wind whipped up. Before anyone could tell what was happening, a tornado took hold of the meadow and roared with a fury like none of the animals had ever heard.

As quickly as the storm took hold, it started to subside, and the sun peaked out from a cloud. All of the animals poked their heads out of their homes and hiding spots and wondered if it was safe to come out? Together they said, "Zebu what do your pinned ears say? Is it safe? Can we come out?"

Baby Zebu responded, "all is clear, the storm has passed, everyone can come out. It is safe."

All of Zebu's friends came up and thanked him for letting them know
early to take cover. If baby Zebu had not warned them, many of his
friends would have been in the meadow when the storm and tornado
had hit, and they would have been hurt. His friends said to him,
"Zebu those pinned ears of yours are very special."

Baby Zebu beamed and felt very special. He was proud of himself. He had no idea that his pinned back ears were so special. Because of them, he was able to warn all of his friends about the dangerous storm, and he could keep everyone in the meadow safe.

Baby Zebu thought to himself.... I wonder what my next adventure will be with my pinned back ears?

www.ingramcontent.com/pod-product-compliance
Lightning Source LLC
Chambersburg PA
CBHW040212240726
48664CB00002B/922